busy baby animals

deer

Please visit our web site at: www.garethstevens.com
For a free color catalog describing Gareth Stevens' list of high-quality books
and multimedia programs, call 1-800-542-2595 (USA) or 1-800-461-9120 (Canada).
Gareth Stevens Publishing's Fax: (414) 332-3567.

Library of Congress Cataloging-in-Publication Data

Johnson, Jinny.
    Deer / by Jinny Johnson; [illustrated by Ch'en-Ling; photography by Susanna Price].
  —North American ed.
      p. cm. — (Busy baby animals)
    ISBN 0-8368-2922-0 (lib. bdg.)
    1. Deer—Infancy—Juvenile literature. [1. Deer. 2. Animals—Infancy.]
  I. Ch'en-Ling, ill. II. Price, Susanna, ill. III. Title.
  QL737.U55J64   2001
  599.65'139—dc21   2001020533

This North American edition first published in 2001 by
Gareth Stevens Publishing
A World Almanac Education Group Company
330 West Olive Street, Suite 100
Milwaukee, Wisconsin 53212 USA

This U.S. edition © 2001 by Gareth Stevens, Inc. Original edition © 2000 by
Marshall Editions Developments Ltd. First published by Marshall Publishing Ltd.,
London, England.

Illustrations: Ch'en-Ling
Photography: Susanna Price
Editor: Elise See Tai
Designer: Caroline Sangster
Gareth Stevens editor: Katherine J. Meitner
Gareth Stevens cover design: Katherine A. Kroll

Printed in the United States of America

1 2 3 4 5 6 7 8 9 05 04 03 02 01

busy baby animals

deer

Jinny Johnson

Gareth Stevens Publishing
A WORLD ALMANAC EDUCATION GROUP COMPANY

As soon as she
was born, Dama
struggled to her
feet and followed her
mother. Her legs were
weak and wobbly.

At first, Dama could not walk very far.

When her mother went to find food, Dama hid in the leaves to keep safe.

Now that Dama is stronger, she can run. When she gets lost, she bleats, and her mother finds her.

Dama drinks
her mother's
milk and
nibbles on food.

She likes to eat
grass and leaves.

Dama loves to run and play. Her big ears and sharp eyes tell her when danger is nearby.

13

Deer eat during the day and at night. When they are not eating, they nap.

Dama is tired now.
Sleep well, Dama.

More about Deer

Fallow deer originally came from southern Europe and the Middle East, but now they can be found in many places around the world. Most fallow deer live in woodlands and parks, where they eat grass, leaves, nuts, and berries. Females live in herds with their babies, while males live together in separate groups. Adult males grow a pair of broad, flat antlers each year. They use them for fighting rival males during the breeding season. In spring, they shed their antlers to grow a new, slightly larger pair.